CLASSROOM
ASSESSMENT
FOR STUDENT
SUCCESS

The Author

Richard J. Stiggins is founder and president of the Assessment Training Institute, an agency that provides educators with professional development in using assessment for instructional intervention. Stiggins has served as a school district assessment director, director of test development for the American College Testing Program, and director of the Centers for Classroom Assessment and Performance Assessment at the Northwest Regional Educational Laboratory in Portland, Oregon. His fifteen years of classroom assessment research is summarized in his book *In Teachers' Hands: Investigating the Practice of Classroom Assessment* (1992). He has translated the results of that research into practical strategies for teachers in his handbook *Student-Centered Classroom Assessment*, 2nd ed. (1996). He has also produced 20 assessment training videos.

Student Assessment Series

CLASSROOM ASSESSMENT FOR STUDENT SUCCESS

Richard J. Stiggins

Glen W. Cutlip
Series Editor

nea
NATIONAL EDUCATION ASSOCIATION

Library of Congress Cataloguing-in-Publication Data
Stiggins, Richard J.
    Classroom assessment for student success / Richard J. Stiggins.
        p. cm.—(Student assessment series)
    Includes bibliographical references.
    ISBN 0-8106-2071-5
    1. Educational tests and measurements—United States.
    2. Motivation in education—United States. 3. School improvement
    programs—United States. I. National Education Association of the
    United States. II. Title. III. Series.
    LB3051S85344 1998
    371.26—dc21   98-39535
                                                                 CIP

CONTENTS

INTRODUCTION

The field of student assessment—from methodology and techniques to the use of results—is changing, and these changes are dramatically affecting the work of education employees.

On one hand, these changes have created new options. For example, classroom assessment instruments have expanded to include assessments based on portfolios, projects, and performances. Teachers now assess a student's performance based on predetermined criteria more closely aligned with the instructional objectives of the lesson and tailor instruction more specifically to individual students. Students become partners with the teacher in assessment by having access to these criteria at the beginning of the lesson. Classroom assessment is truly becoming an integral part of the instructional program as more and more teachers add these assessment techniques to their repertoire.

On the other hand, changes in student assessment have created new concerns, especially in the use of assessment results. Today, assessment results are being used for more than comparing an individual student's performance against a state or national norm, and for more than providing data for making program improvement decisions. They are being used to determine the success or failure of teachers and schools. Policy makers and others are using large-scale assessments to decide whether teachers and schools are providing an adequate education to all students and attaching consequences, positive and negative, on the basis of student assessment results. The use of student test scores has raised the stakes for all education employees.

Consequently, student assessment is part of every teacher's work. In fact, nearly one-third of a classroom teacher's time is spent assessing and evaluating students. Many influential groups have identified competence in student assessment as essential for the training and licensing of new teachers and the upgrading of the skills of practicing teachers (National Board for Professional Teaching Standards, Interstate New Teacher Assessment Consortium, National Council for Accreditation of Teacher Education, Educational Testing Service, and the National Association of State Directors of Teacher Education and Certification). These groups estimate that less than one-half of currently practicing teachers have received adequate training in student assessment.

To help members and other educators keep abreast of the ever-changing field of student assessment, the National Education Association (NEA) commissioned leading assessment experts to write about student assessment from their perspectives. Expert Richard J. Stiggins, the author of this book on classroom assessment for student success, proposes a plan for educators to expand their vision of the relationship between assessment and effective schools and provides a map to help them move from current ways of assessing to the expanded vision. He encourages educators to become a part of the process of helping their school or district use assessment to promote student achievement. The book is intended to be of use to teachers at all levels, preschool through graduate studies, as well as to other education employees.

The NEA developed the Student Assessment Series to help teachers and other education employees improve their knowledge and skills in student assessment and hopes readers will find the series a valuable resource for current and future student assessment practices.

Glen W. Cutlip
Series Editor

RELATING ASSESSMENT
TO EFFECTIVE SCHOOLS

Those of us who grew up in the 1950s, '60s, '70s, or '80s were not reared in the healthiest of assessment environments. In many cases, we were left to guess what achievement targets were going to be covered on upcoming tests. We were left to "psych out" what the teacher expected. We took standardized tests that reflected achievement targets that were a mystery to all concerned—students, parents, and even teachers. No one seemed to understand the meaning of the resulting scores.

Our teachers were told that the multiple choice test was the best way to measure student achievement. So they were directed to transform all of their achievement expectations into this format, whether it made sense to do so or not. But, they were given little or no training on how to do this. We grew up in an assessment environment in which teachers were not expected to know how to assess the achievement of their students.

We attended high schools that presumed to describe the entirety of our academic attainments, including all that we learned across four years of all those different subjects, in the form of a single three-digit number with a decimal point—our grade point average. And then, acting at the behest of colleges, they reduced us even further to a "rank in class." Our goal, we were told, was to finish high in the rank order—by whatever means.

But why, you might be asking yourself, has he written the previous paragraphs in the past tense? Has any of this changed in the 1990s? Do our students experience a different kind of assessment world today? While it is tempting to conclude that little has changed, I think there is compelling evidence that a new kind of assessment world—a far more positive and productive assessment environment—is emerging. Consider the evidence.

Over the past decade, we have learned to put our achievement expectations in sharp focus. We possess far clearer understandings today than ever before about what it means to be a proficient reader, writer, math problem solver, student of science, critical thinker.

These refined standards of academic success are being translated into statewide tests that differ from the standardized tests we took during our school years. Their targets are far clearer to all concerned. As a result, the test scores are far more useful to administrators and policy makers today.

In addition, we have come to understand that we can choose from a much wider variety of assessment methods than just multiple choice tests. We know, too, how to develop and use both objectively and subjectively scored assessments to produce dependable information about student achievement. In short, we can differentiate very clearly between sound and unsound assessment and grading practices. We know, too, how to train educators to meet standards of assessment quality.

Further, we now understand how to communicate effectively about student achievement using far more than just test scores and report card grades. Increasing numbers of teachers are relying on portfolios and various student/parent/teacher conferences to deliver messages about student success.

We are becoming very sophisticated at weaving day-to-day classroom assessment into the teaching and learning process. For example, we can open up the assessment design and development processes and bring students in as full partners, thus turning assessments into powerfully focused and highly motivational learning experiences.

In short, we are poised to emerge from the counterproductive assessment environments of our youth into an array of assessment applications that will be far more constructive for students. But to make this transition, we have work to do.

The purposes of this book are to explore that scope of work and to:
- expand your vision of the relationship between assessment and effective schools
- map a journey from where we are now in assessment in American education to the expanded vision
- encourage you to become part of the process of helping your school or district use assessment to promote student academic well being.

If the book is successful, you will arrive at the final pages with a strong desire to learn more about assessment as a teaching and learning tool. In that case, the annotated list of references provided in Appendix A will guide you.

Let's start with a more complete look at our collective assessment history and then build a bridge from there to a far more promising assessment future.

Assessment Traditions

Over the decades, schools and communities have endeavored to forge strong bonds between assessment and effective schools. Assessment has become both a stimulus for and the indicator of the impact of school improvement efforts.

Bond #1: Assessment for Public Accountability

Historically we have tried to make assessment a stimulus or driver for change through our traditional use of standardized achievement tests for public accountability purposes. A community periodically directs its educators to administer an objective, third party assessment of student achievement so parents and taxpayers can see evidence that teachers are doing the job they have been hired to do—promote student achievement.

Further, communities almost always accompany this testing requirement with a firmly stated expectation that the scores reported be high.

This conveys a subtle but forceful message that teachers and administrators had better work hard and present quality programs in order to avoid the public embarrassment of low test scores. The not-too-hidden belief is that schools will be most effective if communities keep the heat on through the threat of public accountability. In other words, taxpayers and policy makers often operate on the assumption that low standardized test scores mean educators are not working hard enough. Educators, in turn, do work hard to promote high achievement that can be reflected in these periodic test scores.

This leads to a second attempt on the part of educators to bond assessment and effective schools.

Bond #2: Assessment for Program Planning

In the service of achieving high scores, school personnel commonly analyze the test scores for clues as to how to be more effective, to determine whom to help and how. We routinely disaggregate scores on the basis of student demographics and examine item analyses as we attempt to find a higher resolution portrait of strengths and weaknesses.

Without question, important insights often come to those who take the time to look—insights that can improve the quality of schools. For example, we can identify subsets of our student population in need of greater resources. Further, we can find particular components of our instructional programs that do not prepare our students to answer particular kinds of questions correctly.

Going Out of Balance

While these first two bonds between assessment and quality schools have been productive, however, they also have given rise to a serious problem. Policy makers have become obsessed with the belief that standardized tests alone can drive schools to excellence. This kind of thinking has become so dominant that it has caused us to lose perspective on the potential value or importance of standardized tests.

Our fascination with the power of standardized tests began in the 1940s with our first national college admission testing programs, SAT and ACT assessment. Regardless of their intended purpose, both turned into accountability tools, and the rise and decline of average test scores brought national media attention. Even today, we continue to think of test scores as indicators of the health of the American educational system.

In the 1950s we added the first commercially available norm-referenced standardized achievement test batteries. And in the 1960s, with the birth of the accountability movement, we witnessed an explosion in the use of these tests in districtwide standardized testing programs. All or most of these programs remain in place today.

In the 1970s, we added statewide testing programs, beginning the decade with three and ending it with three dozen. Today that number has grown to forty-eight.

The 1970s and 1980s brought the addition of the National Assessment of Educational Progress. Finally, starting in the 1980s and extending through the late 1990s, international assessments have been used as a basis for competition in the hope that the risk of worldwide embarrassment will promote hard work by America's educators.

We have witnessed the addition of layer upon layer of evidence of the strength of our belief that good tests make good schools. Notice that the progression moves further and further from the seat of the educational process, the classroom. In fact, when scientists recently reported the possibility of life on Mars, I began to wonder if interplanetary assessment might be far behind!

My point is *not* that these various standardized tests are bad or inappropriate. Without question, they serve valuable purposes. They can provide information about student achievement that can inform important programmatic and policy-level decisions. But one need only reflect upon the billions of dollars spent on standardized testing across all these levels over the past five decades to understand the strength of our collective belief that such large-scale tests will lead us to the promised land of school improvement.

The Heart of the Problem

Reason suggests, however, that while such tests can help improve schools, they are far from sufficient if our goal is excellence in education. They are insufficient because periodic standardized tests fail to meet the information needs of three critical groups whose decisions bear directly on the quality of the schooling experience: students, teachers and parents.

Assessments occurring once a year are not likely to help a teacher who makes a decision on average every three to four minutes or a student who must decide every day what to do to succeed. Assessments that portray achievement in broad strokes will not serve teachers who need high-resolution pictures of student strengths and weaknesses. Nor are assessments that supply results several weeks or months after the test is administered likely to meet the needs of those who have to decide what to do in the classroom right now.

This is why teachers, students, and parents rely on evidence of student achievement generated day to day through the use of the classroom assessment process. But here is the paradox we must face: As a society, we have invested billions in the service of ensuring the quality of our standardized tests. But how much have we been willing to invest to ensure the quality of the day-to-day classroom assessment process—the other 99.9 percent of the assessments that happen in a student's life? *With a few notable exceptions, we have invested nothing.*

We have been so centered on the naïve belief that we improve schools merely by threatening educators with the potential embarrassment of low standardized test scores that we have failed to see the shortcomings of such tests. Student, teacher, and school success really hinges on the continuous program of classroom assessments that happen in between the once-a-year standardized tests. The paradox we confront is that we have failed to provide teachers with the classroom assessment skills needed to devise quality assessments. Further, we have failed to help them understand how to use those assessments in the service of student success. In short, as a society and school culture, we have been grossly out of balance in our sense of how to use assessment to achieve the excellence we so desperately desire.

As a result, truly effective schools—schools that maximize the effectiveness of the largest possible proportion of their student populations—have remained beyond reach.

Finding a Better Balance

To find a better balance between standardized tests and classroom assessment, we must expand our vision of the relationship between assessment and effective schools to include two important new bonds.

We have been so centered on the naïve belief that we improve schools merely by threatening educators with the potential embarrassment of low standardized test scores that we have failed to see the shortcomings of such tests.

Bond #3: Assessment for Classroom Decision Making

The first new bond centers on the use of classroom assessment to inform classroom-level decision making. Consider the decisions made by students, teachers and parents based on evidence of student achievement generated via day-to-day classroom assessment.

From the day they arrive at school, students look to their teacher for evidence of whether they are succeeding. If that evidence suggests that they are succeeding, a sense of hopefulness begins to grow in them. This internal wellspring of optimism supplies the motivation needed to continue to try, which results in greater achievement, which fuels more motivation, etc., and the result is the upward spiral of a success-oriented student.

On the other hand, if that early evidence suggests to a student that he or she is not succeeding, it may lead them to a sense of hopelessness, which robs the student of the motivation to try, which leads to further failure and less drive.

Next, consider the decisions made by teachers on the basis of classroom assessment evidence: diagnosing student needs, grouping and grading students, pacing instruction, evaluating the impact of teaching strategies, etc. These decisions determine the success of instruction. Again, consider the consequences of basing them on inaccurate information due to poor quality assessment.

Finally, let's not overlook the decisions parents make on the basis of evidence of their child's achievement sent home from these classroom assessments. These are the assessment results that tell parents whether their child needs special help, what kind of help, how to allocate family resources for schooling, whether their child's teacher and school are doing a good job, and whether they are being effective parents. These decisions, too, are critical to student success and thus require sound day-to-day classroom assessment.

If students, teachers, and parents are going to make decisions of this importance on the basis of classroom assessment evidence, we had better be generating dependable evidence of achievement. Imagine the plight of a student making these decisions on the basis of inaccurate information due to a teacher's inept classroom assessment. And what if the teacher and parents also were being misled by misinformation? Yet, historically, we have failed to acknowledge this bond between classroom assessment and school effectiveness and thus have failed to invest the resources needed to assure quality.

Bond #4: Assessment as Instruction

The fourth bond is potentially the most powerful bond. It enables us to use the assessment process itself, along with the scores it produces, as a way to attain greater student success. Let us explore three applications of this idea: student-centered classroom assessment, student-involved record keeping, and student-involved communication.

In student-centered classroom assessment, by opening up the assessment design and development process we create the opportunity to bring our students into it as responsible partners. This represents an excellent way to reveal to students precisely what we expect of them. The result is classrooms in which there are no surprises and no excuses.

In student-involved record keeping, we rely on portfolios or other information management systems to help students stay in touch with and reflect on their own improvement. In this way we enable students to see themselves succeeding as a result of their own efforts. The result is a sense of internal control and academic well-being.

And in the case of student-involved conferences, we assign students responsibility for telling at least part of the story of their own improvement during student-led parent/teacher conferences. This, too, can serve as a source of internal control that can lead to a sense of pride in accomplishment.

We will be ready to take full advantage of the power of assessment in the service of student success only when we are prepared to balance standardized tests used to serve their two intended purposes with high-quality classroom assessments used to serve their two powerful purposes.

Changing Our View of Assessment

Our allocation of assessment resources has been out of balance because we have regarded assessment primarily as a tool of political power and not as a teaching tool.

We have used it to drive change. Operating on the assumption that high-stakes assessment can drive curriculum, we have used district, state, national, and international assessments to force curricular realignment with the test's valued achievement targets. Then, we have used those same assessments to evaluate school success in implementing the new curriculum. We have compelled educators to "drive up those standardized test scores" at all costs, because if they do not, those in visible positions of political power will be embarrassed.

We will begin to achieve the excellence we seek when we replace this simplistic view of assessment as a power tool with a vision of assessment as a teaching tool also. We can use assessment as a way to achieve (not merely drive and then evaluate) the high levels of student achievement we desire.

II. ◆

ASSESSMENT AND STUDENT MOTIVATION

Effective teachers know how to use the assessment process to energize and inspire their students. Unfortunately, not every teacher is effective in this regard. Here's how assessment connected to my motivation when I was a third grader trying to learn to read:

> During reading instruction in Miss Green's third grade class, we took out our reading book, opened to the next story, and took turns reading paragraphs to each other. From the time I started school, I understood that good readers could stand beside their desks and, with their classmates listening, say the words offered in the text out loud in the proper order and with the expression needed to make the story interesting.
>
> Each day Eddie Anderson would start with the first paragraph. Seated alphabetically, we would proceed down his row and then the next, one-by-one reading each paragraph in order. With a last name starting with S, my turn came late in the order.
>
> That was a good thing. I had great difficulty with oral reading. For reasons we did not understand then but do understand now, I had (and continue to have to this day) difficulty connecting my eyes and my mouth. So I would stammer, leave words out, insert the wrong words, and lack all expression. Most embarrassing! But, there was no escape.
>
> In order to manage those risks, I devised a crafty strategy.

A quick aside: After spending the past two decades studying classroom assessment processes I have concluded that, from the student's point of view, classroom assessment is about risk management. Students consistently ask themselves, how can I avoid the embarrassment of being seen as incapable as a learner? The more completely we understand their risk management strategies the more thoroughly we will understand how to motivate them to want to succeed. But back to my story. Here was my risk management strategy in third grade:

I'd quickly count the students present in class, then count down the paragraphs, find my paragraph and practice—so I wouldn't make too much of a fool of myself.

Sometimes my plan would backfire. If someone had a short paragraph, Miss Green might ask that student to read a second one. Oops—the best laid plans... I would have to quickly recalculate and practice anew. Or other times, Teri Smith, the girl right in front of me, would read two paragraphs on purpose—just to set me up! Payback for that incident on the playground. Or still other times, Miss Green would call on us in random order, so I couldn't practice. My worst nightmare... literally!

But even more troubling was her practice of asking comprehension questions during the reading. When she would call on me for an answer, I never knew it because I had not been listening. I had been practicing.

I was labeled a very poor reader. And according to the definition of good reading applied in that classroom, that was a correct label. I received low grades in reading, and regular messages found their way home to Mom and Dad about my poor reading performance.

My dad, a very hard-working man, was convinced that I was failing because I just wasn't trying hard enough. He told my teacher, "Just send the work home, and I'll see that he does it or else ..." But he was wrong. I was trying. I was desperate to overcome this problem.

Another aside: This is akin to the point of view I mentioned in the opening chapter on the part of policy makers who assume that if schools are not working, it is because teachers and administrators simply are not working hard enough. Just turn up the heat, they contend, and things will improve. The problem is that inducing fear when the victim does not know how to improve (that is, has no capacity to respond) does not result in greater learning. It results only in increased anxiety, frustration, and sense of futility. Does that sound like a solid foundation for learning? I think not! But that is exactly what happened to me.

Eventually, I came to believe I would never be a good reader. A sense of futility set in and I stopped trying. As a result, I knew that future embarrassment was inevitable and I came to hate reading. It was far safer for me to become ill just before reading and request a trip to the school nurse (risk management).

The consequences of my internal sense of failure were long-lasting. I avoided reading of all sorts (including comic books!) throughout elementary school, and just muddled through literature topics in junior high and high school. As a direct result of the classroom assessment process in the earliest grades, I thought I was incapable of reading, couldn't do anything about it, and found ways to manage the risks.

I have a confession to make to my high school English teachers. I wrote four book reports in high school. They were all about the same book—*Lord Jim*—and I never read the book! Cliffs notes—my risk management strategy.

It was not until I was in college that I had the breakthrough that permitted me to find the joy and power of reading—to find that I had been wrong for all those years. I can read and learn and thoroughly enjoy the process—just not fast and not aloud.

Note the progression that unfolded here. Non-achievement led to poor performance on assessments and low grades, which, in turn, led to a sense of futility on my part and ultimately to my giving up. The point in telling this story is not to indict Miss Green for doing a bad job. She had a vision of reading success and assessed it well. It does matter that her vision of what it meant to be a good reader was far too narrow. And her way of teaching reading, we now understand, was not the most effective. To be sure, these factors influenced the results.

But, I want us to redirect the focus of our attention away from the teacher toward how I—the learner—used the classroom assessment process to make critically important internal decisions that had long-term implications. Herein lies the crucial bond between assessment and student motivation that we must come to understand.

The essential question is: How can we help our students want to learn? I submit that the classroom assessment process can provide that motivation if we use it smartly. The goal must be to use the assessment process to energize and inspire students—not to turn them off by causing them to come to hate reading or math or science.

Student Motivation Traditions

Consider the bond between assessment and student motivation that characterized the classrooms in decades past. Historically, how have teachers used assessment to motivate students? They have relied on test scores, report card grades, and promotion as rewards and punishments to encourage or cajole students into behaving in academically responsible ways.

The message was this: Work hard and learn a lot and you will receive high test scores. Fail to do so and you will be given low test scores. Accumulate enough high test scores over time and you will be given high grades. Fail to compile a record of such scores and you will receive failing grades. Achieve enough high grades and you will be promoted to the next level. Fail to collect grades that are high enough and you will be retained.

Think about the psychological forces at work here—reward and punishment. The motivational system is based on behavior management, on operant and respondent conditioning. Remember the photographs in your introductory educational psychology textbook of pigeons pecking dots to get seeds and rats pressing levers to keep from being shocked by the steel grid in the bottoms of their cages?

We have tended to regard grades as seeds and shocks. If we manage schedules of reward effectively, the "reinforced" behavior will continue to be exhibited. So, we reinforce academically responsible behavior or its apparent consequences. If we use punishment judiciously, we can "extinguish" undesirable behavior. So we endeavor to extinguish counterproductive behaviors.

The problem with this form of motivation, however, is that students are considerably more complex organisms than pigeons and rats. They can reason in very complex ways and figure out how to act in their own apparent best interests.

Therefore, when they see their own best interests being served by getting high grades, they will perform accordingly. And sometimes, offering a valued enticement (gold stars or points to accumulate for a pizza) or helping them to understand a potentially negative consequence of inaction (no recess) will lead them to see the self-interest. If we can use rewards and punishments to encourage students to engage in activities they might not otherwise experience, without doubt they can benefit.

We must be careful not to blithely assume that behavior management works this simply all the time. Even when it appears to be working, some unfortunate side effects can emerge. These are some of the reasons why we must begin to think more deeply about the relationship between assessment and student motivation.

One such problem arises when the grade becomes a light so brilliant in the student's eyes that he or she cannot see beyond it to understand the required achievement. Depending on that grade, the student (perhaps a third grade reader) can learn to hate the very form of achievement we want him or her to love. But more importantly, if that light becomes too brilliant and the student comes to believe that grades must be high regardless of the cost, that student might turn to cheating and misrepresent his or her real achievement. Aside from the moral implications of such behavior, consider the consequences for the amount that student will learn. Incidentally, reports of the extent of cheating in our nation's high schools suggest that is a very real side effect.

Another side effect arises when the grade becomes the monetary system of the classroom. In this case, students come to believe they deserve a high grade because they worked hard on a project, regardless of the quality of work or the amount they learned from doing it. We see this play out when students say, "If you aren't going to assign a grade for doing it, it's not worth doing. I'm just not going to do it." Consider the implications of this for student learning.

Yet another side effect plays out when grades cause students to minimize their risk taking. For instance, when students constantly ask, "Is it going to be on the test?" they are trying to find the limits of our expectations so as to play it safe. We see that same kind of risk management when high school students opt for easier rather than more challenging courses in order to maintain high grade point averages. I know GPAs are important. But I am simply asking that we think more deeply about the implications of such behavior for the amount these students achieve.

My point is that we are being naïve if we believe we can achieve the academic excellence (maximum learning) we seek merely by treating students like pigeons and rats and by rewarding and punishing them. Even when it appears to work, behavior management may not be working.

On top of this, there are the times when it's obvious that the purely grade-based behavior management system is not working. Consider the student who has been taken to the very edges of her or his capabilities by the teacher. Visualize that student standing on the edge of a cliff overlooking a chasm. Standing beside the student is a teacher saying, "I want you to go beyond this and learn more. So go ahead and leap." There are two instances in which that demand is going to threaten the student.

The first is when that student cannot see the other side of the chasm. This happens when the student has no idea what the new achievement target is that the teacher wants him or her to attain. The other happens when the student can see the other side, but retains a personal sense that the distance is just too far, the gap just too wide, and that it's hopeless even to try. In both cases, in the child's mind, failure is inevitable.

Thus, both instances lead us once again to a risk management dilemma for the student: "If I leap, I might disappear down the chasm—just like last time. And it hurts to hit the bottom! But if I don't, I fail anyway. Maybe I should distract them by acting out in some very disruptive way. Or maybe I should cheat and fool them into thinking I leaped. Or maybe I should just leave and avoid the whole problem…" How many times does a primary grade student need to trust his or her teacher and take the leap, only to crash into the bottom of the chasm yet again, before concluding: "Hey, this isn't working, is it? I must be too dumb to learn." What are the likely consequences for that student's motivation to strive for academic excellence?

How do we remove learners from this dilemma without removing the requirement that they learn and grow? I'd submit to you that the answer resides in the way we use the classroom assessment process to help them find the internal motivation they need to risk trying to grow.

A Wellspring of Student Motivation

When students are confident, they have the inner reserves to permit themselves to venture to the edge of their comfort zones. On the other hand, when they lack confidence, they tend to withdraw within their comfort zones and are unwilling or unable to behave in ways that might further damage their confidence.

The teacher's instructional task is to take his or her students to the edges of their capabilities so they can grow from there. But the teacher's instructional challenge comes in two parts. The first is to help each student arrive at the edge still in possession of the confidence needed to risk the failure that might result from an attempt to go even further. The second is to let students know that, when we grow, at first we may fail and that is all right. We must stop delivering the message to students that failure is a bad thing. Failure is inevitable, especially when we are trying to grow. Wise teachers can use the classroom assessment process as an instructional intervention to teach these lessons.

Here is another way of capturing that same thought: Anyone can use the classroom assessment process to destroy a student's confidence. We could probably spend an emotional afternoon sitting around telling personal stories about how this was done to us during our youth. But can we get past this as teachers? Are we good enough to use the classroom assessment process to maintain or even build student confidence—especially once it has been destroyed? I refer here to the creation of an assessment world that is the antithesis of the one in which most of us grew up.

Student-centered class-room assessment opens up the assessment process and brings students in as partners in monitoring their own level of achievement.

We can use the assessment process to help students bridge the apparently large gulf between where they are and where we want them to be by means of student-centered classroom assessment, student-involved academic record-keeping and student-involved communication about their own success as achievers. Let me explain how these work.

Student-centered classroom assessment opens up the assessment process and brings students in as partners in monitoring their own level of achievement. Under the careful management of a teacher who has a vision of what she wants her students to achieve, students are invited to play a role in defining the criteria by which their work will be judged. They learn to apply those criteria to the evaluation of their own practice work. And they collaborate to apply those standards to the work of their classmates. In short, we use student-involved assessment to help them understand our vision of the meaning of their academic success. The result is class-rooms in which there are no surprises and no excuses.

Student-involved record-keeping brings them into the process of monitoring changes in their performance over time. One way to accomplish this is by having students build portfolios of evidence of their success and by requiring periodic self-reflections about changes they see. In effect, we use ongoing student-centered class-room assessment as a mirror to help students watch themselves grow. This can be a powerful confidence builder by enabling them to feel in control of their own success.

Student-involved communication brings them into the process of sharing information about their success with their families in student-led parent conferences. When students are prepared well over an extended period to tell the story of their own success (or lack thereof), they seem to experience a fundamental shift in their internal sense of responsibility for that success. The pride in accomplishment that students feel when they can tell their stories well is highly motivational.

In these three ways, we can use student involvement to help them see, understand, and appreciate their learning "destination." This can help our students see our achievement expectations of them as being less imposing. And we can help them find and follow the path to that success destination by relying heavily on continuous student self assessment, which allows them to feel in charge of, rather than victim-ized by, the schooling process. In these ways, involvement in assessment, record-keeping, and communication helps our students build the self-confidence needed to keep stepping off the edges of their capabilities into new learning adventures.

Summary

Our students draw important conclusions about themselves as learners on the basis of the information we provide them as a result of our classroom assessments. They decide if they are capable of succeeding or not. They decide whether it is worth trying or not. They decide if they should have confidence in themselves as learners and us as their teachers—whether to risk investing in the schooling experience.

In this sense, the relationship between assessment and student motivation is complex indeed. We should not be so naïve as to believe that we can force our students to care merely by manipulating schedules of reinforcement and punishment. The downside risk is that such a simplistic system of motivation will turn into a game for them, breeding cynicism, not learning.

The alternative is to find ways to help students learn to respond to more than external motivational forces. We need for them to go on internal control—to learn to take responsibility for their own academic success. We can do this by making them partners in assessment.

And make no mistake, there is much that we teachers must learn to help students find their internal sense of control over their own academic well-being. For instance, we must be crystal clear about the achievement targets we want them to hit. We must know how to develop high-quality classroom assessments of various sorts. We must master the craft knowledge of how to involve students in those assessment-design processes. We must understand the principles of effective communication about student achievement and know how to involve students productively in those processes. We have much yet to explore.

ACHIEVING EXCELLENCE IN ASSESSMENT

To reach the goal of integrating assessment deeply and constructively into the instructional process, we must satisfy five conditions in building assessment environments in schools and classrooms. We must:

1. Build those environments around a *clearly articulated and appropriate set of achievement expectations for each student.*
2. Commit to providing *accurate, understandable, and usable information about student achievement to all key decision makers.*
3. *Understand the differences between sound and unsound assessment practices*; that is, all concerned with the quality of schools must become "assessment literate."
4. Lay a *foundation of assessment policy that demands and supports quality practices.*
5. Reconsider how best to *collect, store, manage, and communicate information about student achievement.*

Let's explore each of these conditions in depth.

Condition 1. Clear Achievement Expectations

To assess student achievement accurately, teachers and administrators must know and understand the targets their students are to master. We cannot assess (or teach!) achievement that we have not defined. To establish clear and appropriate expectations, a school district must take three critical steps.

First, the community and its schools must agree on the ultimate meaning of academic success. Graduation requirements are needed, articulating what students should know and be able to do by the end of high school. The requirements should be based on combined input from several sectors of the community.

Second, district curriculum directors and faculty across all grade levels must decide how the community vision of success can be realized. The result of their deliberations must be a continuous-progress curriculum that specifies how students move through ascending levels of competence from kindergarten through high school to meet the high school graduation requirements.

Third, a careful audit must be conducted to be sure all teachers are confident, competent masters of the achievement targets assigned to them. While districts or communities should not anticipate major problems here, neither should they assume that all teachers are prepared to deliver their part of the vision.

Consider how these pieces come together.

A Vision of Academic Success

Members of a school community do not always agree on the definition of an "effective school." In some quarters, an effective school is a safe place to house children while their families fulfill adult responsibilities. Thus, effective schools serve a custodial function. In other quarters, schools are effective when they rank students from the highest to the lowest achiever. In this case, schools serve a sorting function. And in still other quarters, schools serve to produce competent students, so the most effective schools are those that help the largest proportion of students attain their highest levels of achievement.

These purposes for schooling need not be mutually exclusive. As parents, we demand safe schools because the law demands that we place our children there. Further, in a competitive society where resources for post-secondary education and job opportunities are limited, society asks that students be ranked. But ultimately, an increasingly complex, technically sophisticated society demands that its graduates master the academic competencies needed in order to be productive contributors.

Effective schools are achievement-driven institutions. The more students who succeed in reaching their potential, the better the school. The more sophisticated the achievement targets they hit, the better the school.

This does not mean that all students will experience the same level of academic success. We can never hope for equal achievement because we can never hope for equity of ability. But schools cannot be considered effective merely because they sort students according to achievement, if the result is a rank order of students who have in fact learned very little.

To succeed, schools must find strategies for blending the views of at least four segments of the community. They should solicit the opinions of the *family community*— the parents who entrust their children to schools and the taxpayers who support the social institution. In addition, input must be derived from the *business community*— future employers of those successful graduates. Still other advice must come from the *higher education community*—the other destination for our successful graduates. And finally, careful consideration should be given to the opinions of those in the *school community*—the teachers who are masters of the disciplines students are to learn.

These community segments bring a wide range of background and experience to bear on the question of essential learnings for students. For instance, the family community may bring input from the church. The business community will bring a sense of the future development of a technological society. The higher education community will balance that with a sense of our intellectual foundations. And, the school community will bring the best current thinking about academic standards from within particular disciplines. In addition, the faculty can bring any state-level academic standards to the discussion of local standards.

The process most school districts use to achieve this synthesis of community values is a combination of community meetings and surveys of public opinion. Often several iterations of each are needed to reach a consensus—to work through heated arguments about differences of opinion. Although we cannot take space herein to offer advice on how to make this process work, we know that it is critically important.

Many school districts have succeeded in assembling diverse sets of educational values into composite portraits of their successful graduates. Examples are provided in Figure 1. Although the statement of valued achievement expectations is quite general, it encompasses many essential ingredients.

Figure 1

Examples of High School Graduation Requirements

Successful graduates of our community schools will be:

1. effective communicators, able to read and listen with comprehension, write effectively, and speak clearly in a manner that helps others understand them

2. effective information managers, understanding where and how to access and organize the information they need to meet their personal and professional needs

3. effective problem solvers, understanding how to frame problems in solvable terms and use their reasoning powers to find appropriate solutions

4. able to access and apply technology to assist them in performing the tasks to be accomplished in personal and work settings

5. prepared to function effectively as members of teams, understanding how to contribute to a group effort and provide group leadership when appropriate

6. prepared to be contributing members of a community, taking responsibility for community action when and where appropriate

7. prepared to be lifelong learners, taking responsibility for monitoring their own levels of achievement, planning for personal growth, and carrying out those plans.

A Continuous-Progress Curriculum

Once a community vision of ultimate success is completed, the professional education community must collaborate across grade levels to map out the routes students will take from kindergarten to grade twelve to achieve success.

The result of this work must be a carefully planned and completely integrated continuous-progress curriculum. That means teachers from primary, elementary, middle or junior high, and high schools must meet and divide up responsibility for helping students progress grade by grade through increasing levels of academic attainment. It means that teachers must interact with one another and plan for the contributions to be made by each K-12 team member.

To illustrate, if students are to become competent readers, educators must specify what reading foundations primary grade teachers will need to help their students master. How will elementary teachers then build on that foundation? What forms of reading competence will middle school or junior high teachers contribute? And how will high school teachers top off reading competence that launches confident readers into work or college? Not only must each question be thoughtfully answered, but each teacher must also know how his or her contribution fits into this big picture.

> **A continuous-progress curriculum is the foundation of quality assessment, because it tells us what we should be assessing to track student progress.**

The planning process must be carried out in science, math, reading, social studies, and other disciplines. We must plan for student mastery of content knowledge, specific patterns of reasoning, performance skills, and product development capabilities as they play out within and across disciplines. Planning teams must decide who will take what responsibility for which forms of student growth. If students are to master scientific knowledge, what knowledge must be acquired in early grades? And how will later teachers reinforce and build upon prior foundations?

Many districts have found it useful to work in cross-grade-level teams to generate answers. These planning teams can tap into state standards and grade-level benchmarks to assist in finding appropriate divisions of content. They can also consult the standards being developed by professional associations such as the National Council of Teachers of Mathematics, the International Reading Association, and the National Council of Teachers of English.

A continuous-progress curriculum is the foundation of quality assessment, because it tells us what we should be assessing to track student progress. To create such a program, teachers must meet across grade levels within a local school district and work together as teams.

Roadblocks to Continuous Progress

The development of this kind of integrated curriculum can be tricky for several reasons. Historically teachers have taught alone. Within general curricular guidelines, they have selected their own educational objectives and designed instruction to achieve those objectives.

In addition, communication among teachers has been hampered by a lack of mutual respect across grade levels. Elementary teachers have sometimes found high school faculty controlling, and high school teachers have not always respected the discipline-based expertise of their primary and elementary school counterparts.

Besides, our history of academic freedom has entitled teachers to tailor their own instructional priorities to topics that interest them or represent their strengths. Those who have established personal priorities may be reluctant to reevaluate their emphasis as part of the process of compromise that leads to an integrated curriculum.

For all these reasons, many districts find it productive to precede curriculum-building activities with organizational development in the form of team-building activities.

Constructing a continuous-progress curriculum in the 1990s can also pose some challenging community relations problems. Many who view education from the community assume that we already have a curriculum that is integrated across grade levels. After all, the grade level numbers run in consecutive order and each subject is identified as important in each grade. We hear and make common reference to subsets of this curriculum—"third-grade math," "a sixth-grade reading level," "eighth-grade science," and the like. Parents naturally assume that these labels must mean that a well-planned and articulated sequence of instruction (and therefore assessment) has been laid out for students, with each grade building thoughtfully on those that preceded it. Unless the community understands that such a curriculum has not been developed, they cannot understand what resources are needed to create one.

Teacher Support

With the development of a vision of academic success and a continuous progress curriculum, we establish our expectations of students. Obviously, the next key to their success is our mastery of the targets we expect them to master.

Teachers can neither teach nor accurately assess learning they themselves have not mastered. A school district cannot afford even one classroom where this condition is not satisfied. If just one teacher is incapable of helping students to master essential achievement targets, that teacher becomes a weak link in a chain that will cause some students to fail because they will not have mastered prerequisites.

Consequently, once achievement target responsibilities are divided across grade levels, school districts must be sure teachers are prepared to help students succeed. One challenge in this is to help teachers conduct the open and honest self-reflection they need to evaluate their own preparedness. Most of us did not grow up in an environment where it was safe to admit our inadequacies, and the adversarial tone that often characterizes teacher/supervisor relations has not made it easy for teachers to be frank about their needs for improvement.

Given this history, it is essential that we strive to establish supervisory and professional development environments devoted to excellence—not just minimum competence—in teaching. This takes a kind of collaboration, trust, and confidence that will permit teachers to risk going to their supervisors (in the spirit of professional growth) to ask for help in gaining greater mastery of their discipline. Further, it takes supervisors who will help them get that help without penalizing such open and honest teachers at the next staff evaluation. This kind of growth-oriented environment is essential to help teachers gain the knowledge and skills they need to be confident, competent classroom assessors.

Condition 2. Commitment to Serving All Assessment Users

By definition, an assessment produces results reflective of a particular student's attainment of a specified set of achievement targets at a single point in time. Standardized test results provide achievement data summarized across large numbers of students on multiple targets broadly defined for a particular grade level at some point during the school year. These tests provide periodic status reports most useful at the program-planning level of decision-making.

Classroom assessments, on the other hand, are focused on individual student attainment of targets defined day-to-day or week-to-week during a particular course of study. Because teachers can use repeated assessments, each reflective of the achievement of fewer students, they can observe, understand, and manage the evolution of that achievement.

Educational decision makers who need only periodic access to information reflecting group performance can use standardized test results effectively to satisfy those needs. Teachers, students, and parents who need continuous access to high-resolution portraits of individual achievement are provided that information by classroom assessments. No single assessment can meet the diverse needs of all decision-makers. If we are to administer and use assessments with maximum effectiveness and efficiency, we must plan carefully for their use and understand what information is actually needed.

Understanding Who the Users Are

We find three levels of assessment users in schools: classroom, instructional support, and policy. The first column in Figure 2 describes these categories. Columns two and three identify key questions to be answered and the information needed to help each user. A school district committed to meeting the needs of all assessment users must develop plans for conducting the assessments needed to provide the required information—at all levels.

Instructional staff will obtain the information they need from the teacher's day-to-day classroom assessments. User's needs at the other two levels are served by standardized assessments.

The essential planning question is, How can we be sure all users receive relevant student achievement information in a timely and understandable form? At the classroom level, each individual teacher must develop a plan for answering this question. At instructional support and policy levels, we need a district plan.

Planning for Classroom Assessment

To monitor student achievement effectively and efficiently, all classroom teachers must begin each unit of instruction or course of study with a clear vision of the specific achievement targets their students are to hit. Beginning with the foundational instructional targets, teachers must understand how their students will progress over time to higher levels of academic proficiency. In what order will they master more refined structures of content knowledge? How will they come to use that knowledge productively to reason and solve problems? What performance skills will they master, and in what sequence? What kinds of achievement products will they be called upon to create? In short, at the classroom level, continuous progress curriculum must be mapped.

Teachers also must start their instruction with a predetermined plan for assessing whether or to what extent each student has reached the required goals. Any teacher at any time should be able to provide a written plan for the sequence of assessments to track student progress, and for a status report on the completion of those assessments.

Further, teachers need to weave into their plans a description of how the results are to connect to specific targets in a form understandable to students and parents in time for the decision-making process. Since students, like teachers, make decisions of the sorts identified in Figure 2 on a continuous basis, the feedback plan should also reflect ways to keep them in touch with their own progress all along the way.

Planning for Standardized Testing

Standardized achievement tests, such as those administered on a districtwide, statewide national or international level, are of marginal value to the classroom teacher. Please refer again to Figure 2 (classroom level). As mentioned previously, standardized tests are administered once a year, cover very broad achievement targets, and produce results weeks or months after students have taken them. Thus, they are not likely to meet the needs of teachers who make decisions every three or four minutes, need high-resolution pictures of student achievement, and must have results immediately.

This does not mean standardized tests have no value. These periodic large-scale tests serve the information needs of those who must compare achievement data across many classrooms—that is, those who work at the levels of instructional support, programwide resource allocation and policy setting (Figure 2). Once again, careful planning should guide local practice. In the case of standardized testing, however, that planning must be done at the school district level—not by teachers at the classroom level.

Figure 2
Use of Assessment Results

User	Key Question(s) to Be Answered	Information Needed
Classroom Level		
Student	Am I meeting the teacher's standards? What help do I need to succeed? Are the results worth my investment of energy?	Continuous information about individual student attainment of specific instructional requirements.
Teacher	Which students need what help? Who among my students should work together? What grade should appear on the report card?	Continuous information about individual student achievement.
	Did my teaching strategies work? How do I become a better teacher?	Continuous assessment of group performance.
Parent	Is my child succeeding in school? What does my child need to succeed? Is my child's teacher doing a good job? Is this district doing a good job?	Continuous feedback on the student's mastery of required material.
Instructional Support Level		
Principal/ Vice principal	Is instruction in particular areas producing results? Is this teacher effective? What kinds of professional development will help? How shall we spend building resources to be effective?	Periodic assessment of group achievement.
Lead teacher (mentor, support teacher, dept. chair)	What does this teacher need to do the job?	Periodic assessment of group achievement.

Figure 2 (continued)

Use of Assessment Results

User	Key Question(s) to Be Answered	Information Needed
Instructional Support Level		
Counselor/ Psychologist	Who needs (can have access to) special support services such as remedial programs? What students should be assigned to which teachers to optimize results?	Periodic assessment of individual achievement.
Curriculum director	Is our program of instruction effective?	Periodic assessment of group achievement.
Superintendent	Are programs producing student learning? Is the building principal producing results? Which programs need/deserve more resources?	Periodic assessment of group mastery of district curriculum.
Policy Level		
School board	Are students in the district learning? Is the superintendent producing results?	Periodic assessment of group achievement.
State department of education	Are programs across the state producing education results?	Periodic assessment of group mastery of state curriculum.
Citizen/ Legislator (state or national)	Are students in our schools achieving in ways that will allow them to be effective citizens?	Periodic assessment of group achievement.

The questions that must guide the administration of standardized tests at instructional support and policy levels are like those that teachers must ask about their classroom assessments. What standardized tests are to be administered at what grade levels, reflecting what achievement targets at what point in time? Further, who are the specific assessment users to be served by the results?

A careful analysis of standardized tests currently in use within the school district should reveal which achievement targets are being assessed and which are not, as well as whose information needs are being met by these tests and whose are not.

If a district administers an annual districtwide standardized achievement battery for public accountability, the district might profile that test in terms of what targets are assessed for what students, when the assessments are administered, and what specific information/decision-making needs are being served. If standardized tests are used for selection of students for special services, which targets are assessed, when are they assessed, and precisely how are the results being used? If the district participates in a statewide assessment, what are the targets tested, at what levels, and for what purpose? Each assessment fills in part of the district's big assessment picture. That big picture might be captured in the form of a table, each row of which profiles a standardized test used in the district in terms of:

- name and form of the standardized test (list each test in a battery separately)
- students tested (grade level and time of year)
- specific achievement targets assessed (content knowledge, specific patterns of reasoning, performance skills, product development capabilities, or some combination of these)
- specific assessment method(s) used
- how the targets assessed (and their results) relate to the district's curriculum
- intended users of results and decisions made based on those results
- procedures for communicating results to all relevant users
- strategies to verify that results have been understood, interpreted, and used correctly.

The big picture of standardized testing that emerges from this analysis will reveal whether and how the results are connected to users. The district leadership team can step back from this comprehensive table and ask:

1. Are there any redundancies in the tests we use? That is, are we paying for multiple assessments to serve the same purposes? Can we eliminate any tests with no loss in the coverage of our testing program?
2. Are there any important instructional support or policy-level information needs not served by our current testing program? Should we be adding any tests to fill those gaps?

Condition 3. Assessment Literacy

The formation of productive assessment environments requires that all contributors become assessment literate; that is, they must understand how to transform achievement expectations into quality assessments. Without assessment literacy, we remain unable to gather and use accurate information about student achievement.

Even in the 1990s, we remain a national faculty of teachers and administrators who completed undergraduate and graduate training programs almost completely devoid of any of the assessment training needed to do our jobs. Only a handful of states require competence in assessment as a condition to be licensed to teach. Only three states explicitly require competence in assessment as a condition for certification as a principal. As a result, in many schools and colleges of education there is little interest—let alone skill—in addressing this critical aspect of professional competence. So it falls to local school districts to rely on in-service programs to fill the gap.

We prepare teachers to develop and use sound classroom assessments when we teach them to apply the six criteria below in judging the quality of any assessment. It must:

- arise from and reflect clear achievement targets
- arise from and promise to serve clearly articulated purposes (users and uses), including the purpose of motivating students
- rely on proper assessment methods capable of accurately reflecting the desired target
- sample student achievement in a manner that leads to confident conclusions about that achievement
- control all relevant sources of bias that can distort assessment results
- be transformed into timely and understandable communications about student achievement.

We are assessment literate when we know and understand what each of these means and when we can apply them in our own learning environment, be it a classroom, department, building, district, or state.

Condition 4. A Supportive Policy Environment

Another important part of a quality assessment program is a statement of commitment to quality from those in school district leadership positions. That statement should make the standards of sound assessment practice clear and understandable, spelling out who is accountable for meeting those standards. Such a statement establishes the expectation that both teachers and administrators are competent in assessment and that they are expected to demonstrate that competence in daily practice. Policies such as those shown in Figure 3 can guide practice in the proper direction.

The sample policy statement contains an explicit expectation of assessment competence that encourages comprehensive professional development.

Figure 3
Sample School District Assessment Policy

Effective instruction depends on high-quality assessment of student achievement. To meet specific quality standards, (name) District expects that each assessment will:

- derive from a clearly articulated set of achievement expectations
- serve an instructionally relevant purpose
- rely on a proper method
- sample student achievement in an appropriate manner
- avoid all sources of bias and distortion that can lead to inaccurate assessment results
- connect to instruction in ways that maximize student learning.

Any assessments not meeting these standards are to be discarded.

It is the expectation of this school district that all assessments will be directly linked to specific instructional goals and thus to student academic well-being. Two types of use are considered appropriate:

1. providing information for decision making
2. promoting higher levels of student achievement.

Several levels of decision making are considered important to student academic well-being:

- classroom (students, teachers, and parents)
- instructional support (principals, curriculum specialists, support teachers, and guidance personnel)
- policy (superintendent, school board, citizens, and taxpayers).

The district will allocate resources and devise assessment, evaluation, and communications programs to meet the information needs of all these users.

The district acknowledges that assessment can serve as a powerful teaching tool. By involving and supervising students in the assessment and evaluation of their own work, teachers can help them understand the meaning of academic success and meet the highest achievement expectations.

Figure 3 (continued)
Sample School District Assessment Policy

Any assessments that cannot be specifically linked to student academic well-being through effective decision making or instruction should be discarded. In this district, we expect that each will:

- master the knowledge base
- attain appropriate levels of reasoning proficiency
- develop the skills
- master the product development capabilities
- attain the motivational dispositions needed to meet these achievement standards.

District staff will devise an articulated curriculum from kindergarten through high school designed to divide responsibility for helping students make continuous progress toward these targets. Further, the district will create an assessment communication system that permits continuous and thorough tracking of student progress.

Assessment forms considered appropriate for use within this district, Include:

- selected response (multiple choice, true/false, matching, and fill-in)
- essay assessments
- performance assessments (based on observation and judgment)
- direct personal communication with the student.

All staff are expected to understand all these options and know how and when to apply each. In addition, every staff member must know how to use each method to sample student achievement appropriately and how to avoid bias and distortion of results when developing and implementing each method. Given these understandings, staff are encouraged to experiment with innovative applications of these methods in the development of ever more accurate assessments of student achievement.

Personnel Policy and Excellence in Assessment

Several dimensions of personnel policy may be in need of revision to ensure the long-term development of an assessment-literate staff. Beginning at the most general level, state licensing requirements should include explicit expectations of assessment competence as a condition for certification as a teacher or administrator.

Similarly, college programs for teachers and administrators should be encouraged to offer assessment training. Over the decades, higher education has not delivered in this area of professional training.

Admittedly, neither certification standards nor college course offerings are the responsibility of district superintendents. But the quality of teaching is. And superintendents cannot assure their communities of high quality until these aspects of personnel policy change. If we keep pumping new teachers into the system who lack the needed competence, the requirement for local professional development in assessment—often an expensive proposition—will never go away. For these practical reasons, district superintendents might work through their professional associations to lobby state legislatures and higher education to fulfill their responsibilities regarding matters of assessment competence.

Other personnel policy matters hit closer to home. The criteria that districts apply when screening and selecting new teachers and administrators should be adjusted to reflect an expectation of competence in assessment. The criteria used to evaluate ongoing teacher and administrator performance on the job might be adjusted to include evaluation of the quality of assessments and their use. District staff-development policy might be adjusted—at least on an interim basis—to reflect the critical need for assessment training, and assessment and professional development resources might be channeled to fill that need.

In short, leadership must create a local personnel environment that expects and supports competence in assessment, as well as the effective application of that competence in the service of student academic well-being.

Rethinking Other Relevant Policies

In addition to personnel policy, there are other aspects of district policy that may be in need of reevaluation in pursuing excellence in assessment. These include policies governing curriculum, communicating about student achievement, and expenditure of assessment resources.

For example, a school district might codify in both policy statements and regulations its commitment to a continuous-progress curriculum, along with the integration of knowledge, reasoning, skills and product achievement expectations across grade levels.

Regarding policy on communicating about student achievement, it is not uncommon for district policy manuals to be limited to procedures for report card grading and for conducting parent-teacher conferences. These policy statements might be revamped to reflect the expectation that standards of effective communication hold practitioners accountable for formulating clear messages about student achievement, delivering those messages to students and parents in understandable terms, and verifying that the messages have gotten through. Or they may need to be expanded to permit the use of portfolios and various student-involved conference formats.

School district budgets frequently contain just one entry related to assessment: the allocation of funds for the annual districtwide testing program. Since we now understand that assessment occurs at many other levels for many purposes, resources also need to be allocated for these purposes, including professional development to ensure the quality of classroom assessments. Other resources might be needed to create and then maintain an up-to-date information management system for student achievement data.

Condition 5. Effective Management of Achievement Information

If schools are to help students progress in a continuous manner toward ever higher levels of academic proficiency with respect to clearly defined achievement targets, and if teachers are to track their development using classroom assessments, our academic record-keeping strategies will have to evolve rapidly. We must take advantage of modern information-processing technology for generating, storing, and retrieving information about student achievement.

We must take advantage of modern information-processing technology for generating, storing, and retrieving information about student achievement.

In other words, a grade on a report card every ten weeks based on a summary of hand written and often uninterpretable grade-book notations cannot tell the student, teacher, or parent precisely where the student is at any point on the continuous progress path to competence. Moreover, students charged with tracking and communicating their own improvement need continuous access to far greater detail about their own achievement than such records can provide. Teachers, who are expected to take students from where they are to new levels of competence, also require greater detail. Parents, who desire and expect to see specific information about the progress of their children, are not served by grades on a report card every ten weeks. Further, the time required to enter, retrieve, and summarize records by hand, as teachers do with grade books, will prove too time-consuming and labor-intensive to be practical in a continuous-progress curriculum.

For these reasons, school districts must begin to investigate, adopt, and then adapt electronic information management software systems. These systems can assist teachers and districts with essential assessment activities in a number of efficient and effective ways. For example, they can:

- organize the goals and objectives that comprise the curriculum in a continuous-progress manner
- generate assessments using a wide variety of exercise formats
- assist teachers in the collection of classroom observational data
- print assessments for administration or permit their administration online
- permit instant scanning and scoring of selected-response assessments
- allow direct scanning of virtually any form of record desired, such as actual samples of student writing or videotapes of student performance
- provide long-term, dependable, and efficient storage of that information and instant retrieval and summary as needed
- facilitate immediate access to records online by anyone authorized to see them, permitting teachers or parents to obtain instant information about the status of any student or any group of students for conferencing or planning purposes.

Teachers and administrators who use these information management systems can save a tremendous amount of time. Every school district that has not already done so should form an ad hoc committee of teachers, administrators, community representatives, and technology experts to review and evaluate these options. The leadership role in this case is that of supporting professional development so staff understand the time and labor savings these systems can provide, and to help them understand how to involve students beneficially in the use of such systems.

Planning Assessments

Those in school leadership positions can unlock and open the doors to excellence in assessment by ensuring that their leadership teams and faculties ask and answer the questions listed in Figure 4. The answers to these questions show how to develop quality schools through excellence in assessment, where excellence is defined as the balanced and effective use of both high-quality classroom and standardized assessments to promote student success.

Summary

If the goal is to create positive, constructive assessment environments in classrooms, schools, and districts, we must satisfy several conditions. First, we must pour a solid foundation for quality assessment by defining achievement expectations in a manner that helps students progress through ascending levels of academic competence. Second, we must make a commitment to provide all assessment users with dependable information about student attainment of those standards. This requires a commitment to the development of a school community capable of devising quality assessments of those targets. We must become assessment literate.

In addition, we must put in place a policy that supports and demands quality assessment whenever and wherever we use it. And finally, we must plan for and develop information management systems that allow us to remain in close touch with continuous student achievement.

Figure 4

Assessment Planning Questions

Develop a Clear Vision of Achievement Expectations

1. Have our district and community established a set of expectations for successful graduates?
2. Has our faculty worked as a team to take that vision to the classroom in a continuous-progress curriculum?
3. Are we sure all teachers have mastered the achievement targets they expect their students to master?

Commit to Quality Assessment Information for All Users

1. What is our plan for meeting the information needs of students, teachers, and parents using classroom assessment?
2. What is our plan for meeting the information needs of building and district administrators and the community with standardized tests?

Build an Assessment-Literate School Culture

1. What is our plan for evaluating and then building the assessment literacy of district faculty and staff?
2. What is our plan for developing assessment literacy within our community (parents, taxpayers, school board members)?

Develop a Supportive Assessment Policy Environment

1. How will we carry out our review of current policies and regulations to see if they support the effective use of assessment?
2. What is our plan for evaluating existing policies and for identifying new policy areas not currently addressed that will support and encourage the use of quality assessment?

Manage Student Achievement Information

1. What new technologies do we need to effectively and efficiently collect, store, retrieve, and report information about student achievement?
2. How can we investigate currently available information processing systems in light of those needs?
3. How shall we prepare our staff, as well as our curriculum, instruction, and assessment practices, to take full advantage of the efficiency of such systems?

IV.

DEVELOPING ASSESSMENT LITERACY

Assessment literacy includes the abilities to collect dependable information about student achievement and to use that information to maximize student achievement. As noted previously, we maximize the dependability of results when we design assessments to reflect *clear targets* and to serve *specific purposes*—that is, to meet the needs of carefully specified users and uses. In addition, we assure the accuracy of our assessments when we rely on *proper methods*—that is, assessment exercises capable of reflecting the desired targets and when we use those methods to *sample* student achievement in a *bias-free* manner.

We use classroom assessments most effectively when we *communicate* the results in timely and understandable terms, and connect both the assessment process and its results directly to the teaching and learning process.

Let's explore each of these in more detail.

Standard 1. Clear Targets

One starting place for developing a quality assessment is with the specification of the achievement to be assessed. Quality assessments arise from and accurately reflect clearly specified and appropriate achievement expectations for students. We cannot assess achievement that we have not defined.

We must start here because most teachers expect students to achieve in several different ways. The various kinds of achievement differ so fundamentally that no single assessment method can reflect them all. To illustrate the point, here are four types of achievement expectations and ways to assess them.

Knowledge

Sometimes we expect our students to *master* subject matter content, meaning *to know and understand it*. For example, some teachers expect their students to know the causes of the Civil War, understand the entries on the Periodic Table of Elements, develop a sight vocabulary, or learn to spell correctly. Teachers who expect this kind of content to be mastered must be able to specify precisely what content knowledge they expect. Only then can they devise a sound assessment of its mastery.

In the case of content knowledge targets, we can refine our specification even further. We can be masters of content in either of two ways. One is to learn the content outright, so we can retrieve it from memory in an understandable form. Another way is to know where and how to retrieve knowledge from appropriate reference material if and when it is needed. Fundamentally different ways of assessment are required for each kind of mastery.

Thus, the teacher needs to differentiate between content students must know outright to function effectively within a particular academic discipline and content that they must be able to retrieve when appropriate. A second challenge for the teacher is to know how to apply a quality assessment to each type of mastery.

Reasoning

Teachers also want their students to learn to use their knowledge to *reason and solve problems*. Some teachers want to present their students with new problems—challenges the students have not seen before—and have them use knowledge they have already acquired to figure out solutions. This goes beyond merely knowing the times tables in math to being able to apply multiplication algorithms to solve new problems. Other teachers might expect their students to be able to draw appropriate comparisons, reach proper conclusions, or reason analytically—for example, to identify an unknown substance in science class.

The assessment of reasoning proficiency presents its own special challenges that we cannot meet if we do not begin the assessment design process with a clear sense of the patterns of reasoning we expect.

Performance

It is not uncommon for teachers to expect their students to progress beyond just knowing and reasoning to demonstrate mastery of performance skills. We find examples of this in speech class, in foreign language acquisition, as well as in physical education, drama, and science laboratory work. In this case, it is the doing that is important. Achievement takes the form of an actual physical performance.

The key to effective performance assessment is to develop a vision of how high-quality differs from poor-quality performance. Without clear performance standards, sound assessment will remain out of reach.

Product Development

Teachers may expect their students to go even further beyond merely knowing and reasoning to use their performance skills to create products that meet certain standards of quality. For example, we commonly ask our students to write a term paper, build a model of something, assemble a science apparatus, or create a painting or sculpture. We are able to help them succeed in hitting these kinds of targets only when we possess a clear sense of the attributes of a high-quality product.

There is no single assessment format capable of reflecting all of the forms of achievement. To tap them all, we must rely on a variety of different formats. And as it turns out, we cannot select a proper assessment method unless and until we have determined which form(s) of achievement our students are shooting for.

Standard 2. Clear Purpose

Sound assessments are specifically designed to serve instructionally relevant purposes. We cannot design assessments without asking who will use the results and how.

To provide quality information for teachers, students, and parents at the classroom level, we need sound classroom assessments. To provide useful information at the levels of policy or instructional support, we need quality standardized tests. Because of the differences in information needs, we must begin each assessment event with a clear sense of whose needs we are meeting. Otherwise our assessments are without purpose.

There is no single assessment format capable of reflecting all of the forms of achievement.

Suppose I am a fifth grade teacher who wishes to diagnose strengths and weaknesses in the writing proficiency of my students at the beginning of the year, so I can plan instruction around those needs. In this case, I need a high-resolution portrait of the current writing proficiency of each student. In addition, I need assessment results that are comparable across students so that I can identify patterns within the group. And finally, I need the results now—not three months from now.

So I devise a writing assessment specifically tailored to my needs. I have my students write in response to several writing exercises sampling different genre of writing and I evaluate their performance in terms of different elements of good writing (word choice, sentence structure, organization, voice, etc.). With this level of precision, I can confidently profile the writing proficiency of each student.

Now change the context. Suppose I wish to conduct a statewide writing assessment in order to inform the legislature about whether fifth graders in all school districts in our state can write. There are tens of thousands of students to be tested. I don't need the high-resolution portrait. Broad strokes will do. And besides the cost of assessment is a huge issue.

So I select a writing prompt for all students to respond to. I distribute it statewide. The responses come back and I ship them off to a test scoring service to be evaluated holistically—one score for each student. The results come back several months later averaged across all students within each district, revealing how district performance compares. The legislature has what it needs.

The definition of what constitutes a quality assessment is a function of the context within which the assessment is to be conducted. We start the process of devising a quality assessment when we know why we are conducting that assessment.

Standard 3. Proper Methods

Quality assessments rely on exercises and scoring methods that can accurately reflect the intended target while serving the intended purpose. Since we have several different kinds of achievement to assess, and no single assessment method can reflect them all, we must rely on a variety of methods.

The good news is that we have a wide variety of choices at our disposal. The options include *selected response* (multiple choice, true/false, matching, and fill-in), *essays, performance assessments* (based on observation and judgment), and direct *personal communication* with the student. Our assessment challenge is to match a method with an intended target, as depicted in Figure 5. Our professional development challenge is to be sure all concerned with quality assessment understand how the various pieces of this puzzle fit together. We must all know what method to use and when and how to use each well.

This figure is worth careful study, as it represents the foundation of your assessment literacy. Note that all but one of the four kinds of achievement offers assessment method choices and each method connects to more than one kind of target.

To assess student mastery of content knowledge, we can rely on selected response modes of assessment. Each test item examines student mastery of an element of content. But we must begin the assessment development process with a clear vision of what content our students are to master. The essay mode works here too. In this case we can move beyond assessing disconnected elements to assessing students' mastery of knowledge of the relationships among important elements. And finally, we can rely on direct personal interaction with our students, too, when that option is practical; that is, when we have time to use it.

In the case of knowledge targets, performance assessment is a less attractive choice. The reason is that performance assessments almost always ask respondents to use their knowledge in some complex application. Thus, it is possible for a student to be the master of the foundational knowledge needed to succeed, to know how to use that knowledge productively, and still fail the performance assessment. If we inferred from the performance assessment results that the student had not mastered the prerequisite knowledge, we would be wrong. So for purely knowledge targets it is best if we select one of the other three options.

When it comes to assessing reasoning proficiency, however, we have a broad array of options. All four assessment methods can work in this case. But the key to our success is to understand that not all patterns of reasoning can be translated into all the different modes of assessment. Some methods work better in some reasoning contexts than others, so we must be able to align appropriate methods with different patterns.

Figure 5

Aligning Achievement Targets to Assessment Methods

Target to be Assessed	Assessment Method			
	Selected Response	Essay	Performance Assessment	Personal Communication
Knowledge Mastery	Multiple choice, true/false, matching, and fill-in can sample mastery of elements of knowledge	Essay exercise can tap understanding of relationships among elements of knowledge	Not a good choice for this target—three other options preferred	Can ask questions, evaluate answers and infer mastery—but a time-consuming option
Reasoning Proficiency	Can assess understanding of basic patterns of reasoning	Written descriptions of complex problem solutions can provide a window into reasoning proficiency	Can watch students solve some problems and infer about reasoning proficiency	Can ask student to "think aloud" or can ask follow-up questions to probe reasoning
Skills	Can assess mastery of the prerequisites of skillful performance—but cannot tap the skill itself	Can assess mastery of the prerequisites of skillful performance—but cannot tap the skill itself	Can observe and evaluate skills as they are being performed	Strong match when skill is oral communication proficiency; also can assess mastery of knowledge prerequisite to skillful performance
Ability to Create Products	Can assess mastery of knowledge prerequisite to the ability to create quality products—but cannot assess the quality of products themselves	Can assess mastery of knowledge prerequisite to the ability to create quality products—but cannot assess the quality of products themselves	A strong match can assess: (a) proficiency in carrying out steps in product development, and (b) attributes of the product itself	Can probe procedural knowledge and knowledge of attributes of quality products—but not product quality

Stiggins, Richard J., *Student-Centered Classroom Assessment*, 2nd ed., © 1997, p. 81. Reprinted by permission of Prentice Hall, Upper Saddle River, New Jersey.

To assess performance skills, performance assessment is always an obvious choice. In this case, we ask, can students do it or not? One cannot demonstrate the ability to communicate effectively in a second language in spontaneous social interaction (requiring fluent oral communication) using a multiple choice test.

And to see if students can create products that meet certain standards of quality, one must have them create the products. Otherwise, there is nothing to evaluate.

Thus, the assessment method of choice is always a function of the achievement target of choice.

Standard 4. Proper Sampling

A quality assessment provides a representative sample of student performance sufficient in scope to permit confident conclusions about student achievement. All assessments rely on a relatively small number of exercises to permit the user to draw inferences about a student's mastery of larger domains of achievement. A sound assessment gathers a sample of all those possibilities that is large enough to yield dependable inferences about how the respondent would have done if given all possible exercises. Since each assessment context places its own special constraints on our sampling procedures, we must know how to adjust the sampling strategies to produce results of maximum quality at minimum cost in time and effort.

For example, if we expect students to master a body of content covered by three chapters of text, the assessment exercises must cover all three chapters in proper proportions and not be centered on only one or two. If we expect students to become effective speakers of a foreign language, we must sample their skill across a number of communication contexts to be confident of their proficiency.

Obviously, one can reach a point of diminishing returns in sampling student achievement. A major component of one's assessment literacy involves knowing how to achieve a proper balance of comprehensiveness and economy in assessing achievement, whether by selected response, essay, performance, or personal communication. Each method carries its own set of rules for sampling evidence.

Standard 5. Freedom from Bias

Sound assessments are designed, developed, and used in such a manner as to eliminate sources of bias that can distort the accuracy of results. Even if we devise clear achievement targets, transform them into proper assessment methods, and sample student performance appropriately, there are still factors that can cause a student's test score to misrepresent his or her real achievement. Problems can arise from the test, the student, or the environment in which the test is administered.

For example, tests can consist of poorly worded questions, place reading or writing demands on respondents that are confused with mastery of the material being tested, have more than one correct response, be incorrectly scored, or contain racial or ethnic bias within test items.

The teacher can be a source of distortion in assessment results. This can happen any time we rely on subjectively scored assessments, like essays or performance assessments. If scoring criteria are not clear or are carelessly applied, factors other than the student's actual demonstrated proficiency can influence scores. For example, a teacher might be influenced by the student's gender, ethnicity, apparel, or prior performance on similar assessments. These filters cause bias.

> **Sound assessments are designed, developed, and used in such a manner as to eliminate sources of bias that can distort the accuracy of results.**

The student also can be a source of bias. When an examinee experiences extreme evaluation anxiety or interprets test items differently from the author's intent, misleading information about actual achievement can result. Bias also creeps in when students cheat, guess, or fail to take the assessment seriously.

Or the assessment environment could be uncomfortable, poorly lit, noisy, or otherwise distracting—more sources of bias.

To be assessment literate is to be aware of the potential sources of bias and to know how to devise assessments, prepare students, and plan assessment environments to deflect these problems before they impact results.

Standard 6. Effective Use

Assessments are most effective when the results are communicated in a timely and understandable manner and when the assessment process and its results show the learner how to succeed; that is, when the assessment is connected to and thus is part of the learning process. Let's consider the issue of effective communication first.

Communication

Obviously, the foundation of effective communication about student achievement is accurate information about that achievement. Thus, quality assessments form the foundation of effective communication. But we must also understand that the most accurate information in the world is wasted if it is not conveyed in a timely and understandable manner.

Teachers may choose from a variety to methods to convey information to students and parents. Among these are test scores, grades, portfolios, and a variety of conference formats. We can use these options to maximum advantage only when we adhere to one basic principle of effective communication: the message sender and receiver must accept the same meaning of the symbols used to convey information.

Here is an example in which communication breaks down from a parent's point of view:

My child is enrolled in a 10th grade biology course. The mid-term progress report sent home says he is getting a D+ in biology. Yet the only tests and assignments my wife and I have seen have had A and B+ on the top. Josh reports having done all the required work and is at a loss to explain the grade. I request a meeting with the teacher.

At the meeting, I ask the teacher what the progress report means. Without checking the record, he states that my child must not have been doing the work or the grade would be higher. He expresses disappointment that many students don't measure up, but he complains about the lack of time to help students like Josh—given that he faces 180 students each day. I begin to sense that this teacher isn't even sure who Josh is.

I press the issue, asking to see my child's performance records. The teacher uses a computer grade book software program. He enters Josh's name after asking me for the correct spelling and the screen shows a list of entries leading to an average of 69%. The teacher points out that the cutoff scores he has placed in the computer transforms this percentage into a D+. So the progress report is correct.

But as I scan the screen I notice the detail list:

First unit test: 95%
Unit lab report: 85%
Second test: 85%
Unit lab report: 0%

I ask about the 0%. The teacher tells me that if the report is missing, the computer is instructed to enter a zero into the record and into the computation of the grade. But, I point out, Josh seems to be doing very good science, grasping the material very well and performing well on the required assessments. The teacher seems genuinely surprised at the reason for the low grade, agreeing that the rest of the record is very good. How is it, I ask, that the teacher has concluded earlier that Josh is not measuring up? The teacher retreats to the claim of having too little time to know every student.

Later, upon discussing this with Josh, I find that he had specifically asked for permission to turn in the report late, because he wanted to work on the data analysis on our home computer, and the teacher had granted him permission to do so. The teacher, however, has no recollection of that conversation.

The communication process has broken down here. The underlying meaning of the grade is clear to no one. Incorrect inferences have been made about student achievement during the assessment process. This leads to errors in the grade computation process and, ultimately, to miscommunication and misunderstanding about Josh's real science achievement.

Effective communication will occur when the teacher spells out for students the basis of a report card grade, making clear from the very beginning of the grading period exactly what aspects of their achievement will be factored into the grade and how that achievement will be assessed. Then, as the series of assessments is conducted, the teacher keeps students informed about their achievement status in relation to grading standards. Under these circumstances, clear communication is possible, and the message receiver will understand the meaning of the symbol appearing on the report card at the end of the grading period.

Further, we maximize the effectiveness of our communication when we acknowledge that some assessment users need results that contain a greater level of detail than can be provided by a summary report card grade. For example, teachers who receive new students or parents who want to be partners in their child's education may want and need a greater level of precision in the assessment results they receive because they want to diagnose specific strengths and weaknesses. In these cases, we can communicate most effectively when we turn to narrative descriptions of student performance, portfolios containing examples of their work along with student self-reflections, or any of a variety of student/parent/teacher conference formats. If our assessments are accurate and the results are recorded with precision, these alternatives to grades can result in very effective communication.

Connecting Assessment to Instruction

Involvement in the assessment, evaluation, and communication processes can have the effect of placing students in control of their own academic success. Students who are on internal control are more likely to invest the time and energy needed to attain high levels of achievement. This, then, represents yet another potentially valuable bond between assessment and instruction. Teachers who are masters of the craft knowledge of designing and developing sound paper and pencil tests and performance assessments and who know how to bring students into those processes as partners are able to take advantage of student-centered assessment as a teaching strategy. Those who can teach students to monitor the quality of their own work, who can help them reflect upon their improvement, and who can prepare them to conduct parent conferences can use those assessment, record-keeping, and communication processes as powerfully focused instructional interventions.

To meet this sixth standard of quality classroom assessment, teachers must be confident, competent masters of the achievement targets their students are to hit, of the principles of effective communication, and of the craft knowledge of student-involved assessment.

Here is the story of a how a middle school science teacher used the classroom assessment process very productively as a teaching tool:

> A teacher wants her students to learn to prepare high-quality lab reports, because the reports capture the science reasoning processes that students are to master. So she devises a set of lab report performance criteria and runs off a set of rating sheets for her students. But the evening before she is to distribute them, she has an idea.

The next day in class, rather than distributing her rating sheets, she gives her students a lab report of outstanding quality from years gone by. Their homework assignment is to read and evaluate this report, bringing to class the next day a list of elements they think make it of high quality.

The next day, she works with the class as a whole to brainstorm and list on the board key ingredients of successful lab reports. Then she gives them their next homework assignment. She presents each student with a copy of a lab report of dismal quality from years gone by. She tells them outright that it is bad and invites them to read it and tell her why.

The next day, the class brainstorms, again listing on the chalkboard the attributes of a poor quality performance. Then, the teacher has the class carry out a thoughtful comparative analysis of the two brainstormed lists. She asks them to point out the essential differences between the reports. What makes the high-quality report different from the poor one? The students identify six specific ingredients that seem to capture the crucial distinctions: organization, data presentation, quality of scientific reasoning, and the like.

Next, the teacher divides the class into six teams, assigning to each one of the ingredients just identified. The members of each team are to collaborate to complete their homework assignment. They are to (a) define their element in clear and specific terms, and (b) develop a simple three-point rating scale defining a good, poor, and mediocre report in terms of their assigned element.

When this work is completed, each team shares the results of its work for class comment and revision. When all reports have been delivered and all definitions and rating scales adjusted, they return once again to the original two reports. Each class member reads the reports again, rating quality using the newly-developed scales. They compare ratings across the whole class, discuss differences of opinion and, again, adjust the scales as needed.

Notice that the class is several days into this already, and no one has yet written a lab report. A vision of excellence in science reporting is growing here and students are committed partners in this process. They are learning. And by the way, don't be so naïve as to believe that these students are setting the standards. This teacher knows from the outset where this is leading. She has done the rating scales and could hand them out, revealing her expectations to her students. But she has chosen not to. Rather, she has opted to lead them to her vision through a series of inferences enabling them to derive that same vision.

Finally, each student does a lab experiment and writes the first draft of a lab report. Working in teams, they read and evaluate each other's initial drafts using the agreed-upon scales. They provide each other with advice on how to improve quality. Then they revise their work based on this feedback. The feedback and revision process is repeated several times for some team members, as their work progresses up the rating scale.

The teacher reports that the first set of reports is of very high quality, that her students assess well and learn very fast.

Summary

Educators cannot meet standards of assessment quality if they do not know what those standards are or how to meet them. Barriers exist to quality assessments—emotions, lack of time, community beliefs, and lack of assessment expertise. This book is aimed at removing of the fourth barrier—the lack of expertise. Removal of this ultimate barrier is the key to removing personal barriers to quality. Here is why. The reason educators fear assessment and evaluation is that they do not understand it and therefore cannot control it. As they gain assessment wisdom, they gain control, and anxiety dissipates.

Finding time to assess well is difficult when we lack knowledge of assessment tactics that can make the teaching job faster, easier, and better. With assessment literacy comes the time to do the assessment job we were hired to do within the time allotted. Removal of this ultimate barrier is the key.

The reason many local educators have difficulty dealing with assessment concerns in their communities is that they lack the understanding and confidence to address these issues in a forthright manner. So they continue to do what has always been done in testing, regardless of its appropriateness. But the more they know about assessment, the easier it is to help their communities understand what assessment practices are sound. So the development of assessment literacy is the key to removing this barrier.

To determine whether an assessment is going to provide dependable information about student achievement, educators can ask the following six questions about any assessment.

Question 1: Does the assessment arise from a clearly defined target?

Question 2: Does the assessment promise to serve a clearly stated purpose?

Question 3: Does it rely on a method that can accurately reflect the desired target?

Question 4: Do the exercises that comprise the assessment sample student achievement appropriately?

Question 5: Have all relevant sources of bias been accounted for in the development and application of this assessment?

Question 6: Have the results been communicated to the intended user in a timely and understandable manner?

If the answers to all the above questions are yes, then a quality assessment is probably being used. If the answer to any one of them is no, further use should be curtailed. Individuals are assessment literate when they understand the questions, and ask them as a matter of routine.

V.

A PROFESSIONAL DEVELOPMENT STRATEGY

Since most currently practicing teachers and administrators graduated from training programs that failed to impart appropriate levels of assessment literacy, local inservice professional development programs are needed to provide essential assessment expertise. One highly efficient and effective training strategy is presented in this chapter. It places teachers and administrators in control of the development of their own assessment literacy in just the same way as educators put their students in control of the development of their own mathematics proficiency, for example. Reliance on a method for helping adult learners manage their own growth and development is recommended.

Program Objectives

Teachers and administrators are prepared to fulfill their ongoing assessment responsibilities when they:
1. understand essential differences between sound and unsound assessment practices and commit to meeting key quality standards
2. know how to meet standards of quality in all classroom, school, and district assessment contexts
3. know how to use the assessment process as a teaching tool to motivate students to strive for excellence.

Selecting a Training Strategy

To achieve these objectives, educators must design and implement professional development programs that:
- promote a healthy concern for quality assessment by emphasizing its implications for student well-being and teacher effectiveness
- provide practical new assessment ideas and strategies in an efficient manner
- offer opportunities for teachers to experiment in applying those new strategies
- place responsibility for professional growth directly within the hands of each teacher and administrator

- provide collegial support, where educators learn by sharing the lessons they have learned individually
- deliver benefits very quickly to those who apply the lessons learned in their classroom.

To satisfy these requirements, the best professional development programs will rely on a blend of *learning teams* (also referred to as study groups or study teams) and *individual study*.

In contrast, programs that rely heavily on workshops for the development of assessment literacy will not satisfy these requirements. They simply are too expensive, cumbersome, inflexible, and impersonal, and they do not afford teachers the opportunity to experiment with the assessment strategies they are learning about in their own classrooms. Practical application during learning is critical to the adult learning process.

In a study group-based adult learning environment, a small group of five to ten teachers and administrators agrees to meet regularly to share responsibility for their mutual professional development. Between meetings, each team member commits to completing assignments designed to advance his or her assessment literacy. Each member might, for example, study the same piece of professional literature and try the same assessment strategies in his or her classroom, and then return to the group to share and discuss the classroom experience. Or team members might complete different assignments, learn different lessons, and meet to share a more diverse array of insights.

Organizing for Professional Development

The learning team-based method of professional development can be applied in a very flexible manner. Some school districts elect to begin with a *leadership study team* comprised of a few key teachers and administrators from across the district. This team's mission is three-fold, to:

1. develop their own assessment literacy
2. develop and implement a plan for forming and supporting additional study groups throughout the district
3. conduct an ongoing evaluation of the professional development effort to determine its impact.

Others organize learning teams in each building, bringing together interested administrators and teachers. This can stimulate subsequent interest among others in the same building. Learning teams from different schools also might agree to meet periodically in a larger collective effort.

Obviously, learning teams can be configured in any of a variety of ways. Groups might be formed on the basis of grade level (within or across levels) or within or across discipline (math, science, arts, etc.). Learning teams might come into existence as opportunities arise, for example, when an ad hoc committee is assembled to evaluate and consider revising report card grading or when a curriculum-development team decides to deal with some underlying assessment issues. All such instances represent very practical opportunities for developing and immediately applying one's assessment literacy.

Not surprisingly, the key to a productive learning team experience is the first team meeting when team members must make a commitment to growing together. This meeting should be devoted entirely to formulating the group's complete training plan in five specific parts:

1. selecting a meeting schedule, marking all meeting dates on everyone's calendar
2. planning the specific interim assignments that will lead up to each meeting
3. identifying the general kinds of activities to be conducted at each meeting
4. assigning leadership responsibility for planning and conducting each meeting (Some teams have a consistent organizer and leaders; others rely on rotating leadership.)
5. planning the evaluation of team and individual member growth as competent, confident classroom assessors.

> **The key to a productive learning team experience is the first team meeting.**

What to Study

A number of excellent introductory-level books and monographs are available on a variety of important classroom assessment topics and applications. Consider the references listed in Appendix A as learning team possibilities.

Understanding the Time Commitment

For most teachers, interest in learning more about classroom assessment runs very deep. But the tricky part is finding time to learn. And to be sure, the time commitment is significant. For example, the completion of a learning team experience based on the study of the Assessment Training Institute text *Student-Centered Classroom Assessment* (1997; see listing in Appendix A), which provides the operational version of ideas presented herein, will require 35 to 40 hours of personal professional-growth time. This includes time to read, reflect, experiment in the classroom, and share lessons learned with the learning team. It is important to understand, however, that this time commitment can be spread over several months, if the team plans appropriately.

It is tempting to think that training through involvement in learning teams requires that the teacher or administrator invest most of the training time in team meetings. But if that were the case, the learning team options would be no more efficient than traditional workshops—which we already have established as the least efficient of all options.

Make no mistake—learning team meeting time is critically important, but team meetings should take up no more than 25 percent of an educator's time commitment. The remaining 75 percent must be spent in individual study, experimentation, and personal growth. This is why those involved in assessment literacy development must commit (on pain of public embarrassment!) to completing all assignments in between meetings. If they do not, they come to the meetings with nothing to contribute and without the insights needed to benefit from lessons learned by others.

Think for a moment about the important work to be done between meetings. In order to gain access to new assessment strategies, one must study the references describing those strategies. Or one must view and learn from training videos, if appropriate. This takes personal time.

Next, each teacher must allot time to reflect upon the new discoveries and decide which of them might realistically fit into her or his classroom. Specific plans must be developed for experimenting with those new strategies that seem usable. Personal reflection and planning time is important too.

Then comes the classroom implementation, which takes up classroom assessment time. But it is here that the real growth producing lessons are solidified. We see what does and doesn't work, and we adapt new ideas to fit our own students, subject matter, teaching style, and classroom circumstances.

And finally comes the time of preparation for the learning team meeting during which each team member reviews, collects, and summarizes lessons learned for sharing with the group. Often, this might include preparing questions to ask other members of the team for specific help in adjusting some assessment process that didn't work very well. All of this represents the personal work that provides the fuel that makes the team meetings worth attending.

When the team actually assembles, then, it is time to share experiences about what worked, to ask for help, to draw generalizations, to make group decisions about how to explore an idea further. Make no mistake. Important growth occurs here too. But it comes in a more action-packed and compact manner.

Essentially, the power of the study group-based experience lies in the synergy achieved between individual exploration and collaborative sharing. The key to a successful experience is each individual's investment of time. Anyone who is unable or unwilling to invest should not join a team. The actual time commitment will vary, depending on the material being studied.

Now, here is an important school district policy suggestion: If individual teachers and administrators are willing to contribute 75 percent of the time needed to make learning teams work, wouldn't it be appropriate (prudent, a legitimate expectation) for the district to ante up the other 25 percent by paying for team meeting time?

Some districts have covered these costs using time already budgeted for professional development. Others have built schedules in a manner that permitted school to start two hours late one day per week or month. Still others have planned for regular early-release days to give teachers time to meet. Yet another very creative and quite economical option is to rely on the careful use of substitutes for parts of some days, so a team can have time to meet. In addition, it is not uncommon for schools or districts to seek grant monies for this purpose. The promise of time to concentrate on one important topic long enough to internalize some new and useful ideas can be a strong incentive for some. This time commitment, combined with promise of an opportunity to talk with and learn from colleagues (both very rare commodities for most educators), can also be a motivator.

I wish I could find a way to make it quick and easy. I have spent the past two decades trying to simplify the process. But under any circumstances, it takes a personal commitment of time and cognitive energy. So I can only promise that the time and effort invested will pay huge dividends later in terms of much greater student motivation and great time savings. Ultimately, it will make the teaching job easier.

Motivating Participation in Learning Teams

If the promise of time to meet is not enough to encourage participation, other incentives can be woven into the professional development equation. For example, a school district might establish an ongoing working relationship with a higher education institution to offer graduate credits for the successful completion of assessment training through study group work. Assessment Training Institute can offer concrete advice on how to do this (800-480-3060).

We also might look to other, more internal sources of motivation. For example, all learners, regardless of age, are more likely to be motivated to strive for excellence if they have the opportunity to see themselves improving. One way to take advantage of this is to encourage all learning team members to build a portfolio of evidence of their own improvement as classroom assessors. The collection of evidence might include a teacher's journal of self-reflection about his or her evolving assessment competence, actual examples of a teacher's classroom assessments collected over time, and written commentary on the increasing quality of those assessments. Periodically, team members might also conduct *student-led conferences* detailing to the rest of the team their evidence of progress as an assessor. Incidentally, such portfolios could serve as an excellent basis for local university faculty to evaluate the teacher's learning for the award of academic credit.

Yet another way to promote interest in a school building is through the completion of a school wide assessment literacy needs assessment. Appendix B provides the means for doing this in the form of a set of teacher self-rating scales depicting different levels of classroom assessment confidence and competence. Each member of the building faculty might evaluate his or her own levels of performance and then the results might be pooled to reveal gaps in assessment literacy. The next natural activity would be to plan a course of action to deal with those gaps through the development of learning teams.

Evaluating the Impact of Learning Teams

As a faculty develops higher levels of assessment literacy, evidence of the positive impact of the professional development experience will emerge in a number of ways. Some examples that serve as the basis for evaluating the learning process are:
- improved student motivation and achievement in arenas where sound student-involved classroom assessment procedures are being newly implemented
- increased teacher competence and confidence in classroom assessment through the collection of examples of high-quality assessments effectively used

- feedback from students and parents on the quality of the information they are receiving on student achievement
- portfolios showing how team members have increased their own assessment competence, including self-reflections on why and how their assessments have improved
- other recorded evidence of improved classroom assessment quality in the ongoing supervision and evaluation process.

These and other evaluation procedures can provide formative feedback on how to improve the learning team experience over time, as well as summative information about the return on the resources invested in this kind of professional development.

Summary

Instruction is most effective when it includes the use of quality assessments. Such assessments are:
- built around users' needs
- arise from clearly articulated achievement targets
- rely on proper methods
- sample student achievement appropriately
- avoid sources of bias and distortion that can lead to inaccurate results
- are communicated effectively, connecting directly to the teaching and learning process.

Fear of accountability, however, as well as a lack of time and other resources needed to assess well, and community or parent expectations can present imposing barriers to quality. The removal of these potential roadblocks requires the development of an assessment-literate school culture.

Assessment literacy that places control of professional development in the hands of each practitioner calls for an individual commitment to learning about excellence in assessment, at the same time supporting that effort collaboratively. If school districts can support the team effort, motivated educators will ante up the rest.

Remember, this foundation of assessment literacy is only part of a much larger scope of work to be completed within each school district. Assessments are likely to serve us most productively from the classroom point of view if and when we:
- have developed and implemented a continuous progress curriculum within each discipline that ties primary grade achievement expectations to those of high school through all the levels in between
- commit to a set of assessment values that holds the student to be every bit as important an assessment user as is the chair of the school board, allocating resources to achieve balance in our use of standardized tests and classroom assessment
- put in place an assessment policy environment that demands that all concerned with student academic well-being meet specific standards of sound practice, with accountability for all who fail to do so

- collect, store, retrieve, summarize, and deliver information about student achievement using modern information management technologies
- most important of all, understand that we cannot bring our students to the level of confidence and internal control that they will need in order to become productive life-long learners merely by promising As and threatening Fs on their report cards. Rather, we must take them to a place where they don't need us any longer to tell them how well they have done.

APPENDIX A

Suggested Readings for Learning Teams

Basic Assessment Literacy

Stiggins, R. 1997. *Student-Centered Classroom Assessment,* 2nd ed. Columbus, Ohio: Merrill, an imprint of Prentice Hall. A comprehensive teacher's handbook on the development of quality assessments for use as teaching tools in the classroom; distributed by the Assessment Training Institute, Portland, Oregon, along with a Learning Team Trainer's Guide and Case Study Workbook. Note: A free Learning Team Trainers' Guide is available to accompany this text. To order: 800-480-3060, ISBN 3-13-432931-7, $35.00.

The Relationship between Assessment and Student Motivation

Covington, M. 1992. *Making the Grade: A Self-Worth Perspective on Motivation and School Reform.* New York, N.Y.: Cambridge University Press. A comprehensive analysis of the relationship between our evaluations of students and their willingness to strive for excellence. To order: 914-937-9600, Order #34803X, ISBN 0-521-34261-9, $19.95.

Kohn, A. 1993. *Punished by Rewards.* New York, N.Y.: Houghton Mifflin Co. A thoughtful examination of extrinsically and intrinsically motivating ways to encourage students to engage in academically productive work. To order: 800-225-3362, ISBN 0-395-65028-3, $16.45.

Effective Ways to Communicate about Student Achievement

Austin, T. 1994. *Changing the View: Student-Led Conferences.* Portsmouth, N.H.: Heinemann. A teacher's handbook on setting up and conducting student-involved communications. To order: 800-541-2086, Order #08818, ISBN 0-435-08818-1, $14.50.

Davies, A., C. Cameron, C. Politano, and K. Gregory, 1992. *Together Is Better: Collaborative Assessment, Evaluation and Reporting.* Courtenay, British Columbia: Classroom Connections International. A practical guide to the design and completion of student-involved communications. To order: 800-603-9888, ISBN 1-895411-54-8, $16.95.

Performance Assessment Design and Use

Wiggins, G.P. 1993. *Assessing Student Performance: Exploring the Purpose and Limits of Testing.* San Francisco, Calif.: Jossey-Bass. A thoughtful exploration of the role of performance assessment methods in the pursuit of academic excellence. To order: 609-730-1199, ISBN 1-55542-592-5, $30.00.

Using Student-Involved Writing Assessment as a Teaching Strategy

Spandel, V., and R. Stiggins. 1997. *Creating Writers: Linking Assessment and Writing Instruction,* 2nd ed. New York, N.Y.: Addison-Wesley/Longman. A teacher's guide to the integration of student-involved writing assessment with the teaching and learning process. To order: 800-822-6339, ISBN 0-8013-1578-6.

Spandel, V,. and R. Culham. 1995. *Seeing Through New Eyes.* Portland, Ore.: The Northwest Regional Educational Laboratory. Details pre-writing assessment strategies for primary grade teachers. To order: 800-547-6339.

The Practicalities of Classroom Mathematics Assessment

Stenmark, Jean Kerr. 1991. *Mathematics Assessment: Myths, Models, Good Questions and Practical Suggestions.* Reston, Va.: National Council of Teachers of Mathematics. A handbook of assessment guidelines and strategies in mathematics. To order: 800-235-7566, ISBN 0-87353-339-9, $8.50.

Reading Assessment

Valencia, S., E.H. Hiebert, and P. Afflerbach, eds. 1994. *Authentic Reading Assessment: Practices and Possibilities.* Newark, Del.: International Reading Association. To order: 800-336-READ, ISBN 0-87207-765-9, $12.00.

Assessing Student Reasoning Proficiency

Marzano, R., D. Pickering, and J. McTighe. 1993. *Performance Assessment Using the Dimensions of Learning.* Alexandria, Va.: ASCD. Provides many examples of performance assessment exercises and scoring criteria for the assessment of reasoning and problem-solving proficiency. To order: 703-549-9110, Order #61193179, $13.95.

Science Assessment

Brown, J., and R. Shavelson. 1996. *Assessing Hands-On Science.* Thousand Oaks, Calif: Corwin Press. A handbook of performance assessment guidelines and strategies in science. To order: 805-499-9774, ISBN 0-8039-6443-9, $25.00.

Note. All prices subject to change.

APPENDIX B

Self-Evaluation of Classroom Assessment Performance

STANDARD 1: Sound assessments arise from clearly articulated and appropriate achievement targets.

Level 4 (Exemplary)

The school and community have articulated achievement expectations for high school graduates and the faculty has backed those down into a continuous-progress curriculum. I understand how my achievement targets lay the foundation for my students' success in later grades, and I am a confident master of the achievement targets my students are to hit. I also understand how to guide my students through ascending levels of competence during their time with me.

Level 3 (Functional)

The school and community have developed achievement expectations for high schools graduates and the faculty has backed those down into a continuous-progress curriculum. I am adjusting my targets as needed to fit into the agreed upon continuous-progress curriculum and am a master of the targets I want my students to hit. I continue my ongoing professional development as needed to be sure I can lead them to ever higher levels of competence.

Level 2 (Making Progress)

The school and the community are working to develop achievement targets for high school graduates and the faculty is working across grade levels to develop a continuous-progress curriculum. I have identified some dimensions of my achievement expectations for which I may need further professional development. My supervisor and I are planning for my growth. I am on my way toward becoming a confident master of those expectations.

Level 1 (Low Level)

The school and community sense the need for achievement targets for high school graduates. Some of my colleagues on the faculty are uneasy about the lack of connection in the curriculum across grade levels and are aware of the need to develop a continuous-progress curriculum. I probably could use some further professional development in some areas of achievement, but I'm not sure how to do that. Maybe my supervisor could help.

Level 0 (Absence of Quality)

There is no concern about developing a vision of achievement targets for high school graduates or for connections across levels of the curriculum. Neither my supervisors nor I have paid any attention to how my achievement targets might relate to those of other teachers or whether I am a master of the targets that my students are expected to master.

STANDARD 2: Sound assessments are developed to serve the information needs of specific users; that is, they serve clearly articulated purposes.

Level 4 (Exemplary)

I know how the assessments that I develop and use fit into the decision making processes that underpin student success. I have analyzed the specific information needs of students, parents, and other teachers and routinely devise classroom assessment and record keeping strategies to provide the information they need.

Level 3 (Functional)

I am aware of the fact that students, parents, administrators, and other teachers make different decisions on the basis of assessment results and that the information needs of the users of my assessments vary and I plan as best I can to provide the information they need. I keep records of student achievement that reflect the specific competencies students attain and try to help them make sound decisions.

Level 2 (Making Progress)

I am trying to analyze users and uses of assessment and am learning to devise a plan for meeting the information needs of users. I am working on an appropriate record keeping system to get them what they need.

Level 1 (Low Level)

I have thought about the information needs of different assessment users and of the need to maintain records and reporting procedures that meet their needs. But I am not sure exactly how to do so.

Level 0 (Absence of Quality)

I have not thought about or analyzed my own information needs. let alone those of students, parents, or others. I wouldn't know how to proceed in doing so.

STANDARD 3: Sound assessments use assessment methods that accurately reflect the desired achievement targets.

Level 4 (Exemplary)

I know and understand how to align selected response, essay, performance, and personal communication-based assessments with my knowledge, reasoning, skill, and product achievement targets. I know and adhere to standards of quality for each assessment method. As a result, virtually all my assessments rely on methods capable of providing information about student achievement. I experiment with new methods to find better ways to assess. As a result, the full range of appropriate assessment methods is in use in my classroom.

Level 3 (Functional)

I think I understand how to use most of the assessment methods that I have at my disposal to reflect most of my valued achievement targets. I try to adhere to standards of quality for each assessment method. As a result, I select methods that are capable of providing dependable information about desired forms of student achievement. I occasionally experiment with assessment methods to find better alignments with my achievement expectations. I use a variety of assessment methods.

Level 2 (Making Progress)

I am learning how to align assessment methods with valued targets. I am learning how to develop and use each assessment method properly. At least some of my assessments rely on methods capable of providing dependable information about student achievement. I am encouraged to learn about and experiment with assessment methods to better align with my expectations. While such opportunities are rare, I am trying to learn. While I still rely on a narrow range of assessment methods, I am beginning to see other possibilities.

Level 1 (Low Level)

I know I need to align assessment methods carefully with my achievement targets, but I don't yet understand how to make such alignments. I am unsure about the issues of assessment quality for each method. Nevertheless, I hope that at least some of my assessments rely on methods capable of providing dependable information about student achievement. I don't feel comfortable experimenting. Professional development opportunities are rare. I use only a very narrow range of assessment methods in my classroom.

Level 0 (Absence of Quality)

I do not know how or understand how to align assessment methods with their valued targets. I don't question the quality of my assessments. As a result, I don't know if my assessments rely on methods capable of providing dependable information about student achievement. I am unwilling to risk experimenting with my assessment methods to find better alignments with achievement expectations. I adhere rigidly to one or two assessment methods and have no opportunity to learn about others.

STANDARD 4: Sound assessments rely on appropriate samples of student achievement to arrive at confident conclusions about proficiency.

Level 4 (Exemplary)

I know and understand how to develop or select assessments of all kinds (selected response, essay, performance assessment, and personal communication) to include exercises that provide representative samples of achievement expectations. I know how much evidence of student achievement I need to serve my purposes and I rarely waste time gathering too much evidence of proficiency. I act purposefully to make certain all assessments lead efficiently to confident conclusions about student achievement. I strive constantly to refine my sampling techniques.

Level 3 (Functional)

I know and understand how to design assessments of all kinds to include exercises that provide a representative sample of achievement expectations. I try to gather only as much evidence of achievement as I need, and I try not to waste time gathering too much evidence. While my knowledge of sound sampling procedures is limited, I know how to tap resources that can help me learn more.

Level 2 (Making Progress)

I am learning how to design a variety of assessments to include exercises that provide a representative sample of achievement expectations. As a result, I am beginning to analyze my assessments to see if they lead efficiently to confident conclusions about student achievement.

Level 1 (Low Level)

I understand the sampling concept. I am aware of the need to design a range of different kinds of assessments to include exercises that provide a representative sample of achievement expectations. I am attempting to sample student performance in ways that lead efficiently to confident conclusions about student achievement. I still have much to learn.

Level 0 (Absence of Quality)

I haven't thought about sampling issues in assessment. I didn't know I needed to know and understand how to design assessments that include a representative sample of exercises. As a result, I was unaware of the need to design assessments that lead efficiently to confident conclusions about student achievement. My assessments may rely on inefficient and ineffective samples of exercises.

STANDARD 5: Sound assessments are designed, developed, administered, and used in ways that prevent biased results, interpretation, or use.

Level 4 (Exemplary)

I know and understand how to design and use assessments of all kinds (selected response, essay, performance assessment, and personal communication) in ways that control all sources of bias that can lead to inaccurate information about student achievement. I routinely check for and eliminate all sources of bias caused by inadequate assessment procedures, problems arising from within the student, or distractions within the assessment environment before they adversely impact my results. I don't use assessment results that have been rendered inaccurate due to bias.

Level 3 (Functional)

I know and understand most sources of bias that can lead to inaccurate information about student achievement. I don't use assessment results I know to be biased. I try to find and eliminate bias caused by inadequate assessment procedures, problems arising from within the student, and distractions within the assessment environment before they adversely impact results.

Level 2 (Making Progress)

I am actively learning about sources of bias that can lead to inaccurate results. As a result, I am beginning to look for and recognize bias due to inadequate assessment procedures, problems that arise from within the student, and distractions within the assessment environment.

Level 1 (Low Level)

I have minimal understanding of the sources of bias that can lead to inaccurate information about student achievement. I am certain about how to prevent problems. But I am starting to recognize the possibility of bias caused by inadequate assessment procedures, problems arising from within the student, and distractions within the assessment environment. So I want to learn about them.

Level 0 (Absence of Quality)

I don't know or understand how to design and use assessments in ways that control for those sources of bias that can lead to inaccurate results, I am not acting to address the problem.

STANDARD 6: Sound assessments are used in productive ways when results are communicated accurately and effectively and in a manner that motivates students to learn.

Level 4 (Exemplary)

I understand the relationship between assessment/communication and student motivation. I know how to balance the management of incentives with student-involvement in assessment and communication to encourage students to strive for excellence. My students are regularly involved in the self assessment process, and they play key roles in maintaining academic records and in communicating with me and their parents about their achievement. I have an information management system in place to help collect, summarize, and communicate effectively about the competencies of students. I consistently check to be sure messages about assessment results are being understood by users.

Level 3 (Functional)

I have some understanding of the relationship between assessment/communication and student motivation. I rely mostly on the management of incentives to encourage students to strive for excellence. However, my students are involved in the self assessment process, and they play roles in maintaining academic records and in communicating with me and their parents about their achievement. I strive to communicate effectively about student achievement and to check the effectiveness of my communication.

Level 2 (Making Progress)

I am learning about the relationship of assessment to student motivation. I want to know how to involve my students in the assessment, record keeping, and communication processes. And I am striving to improve the effectiveness of my communication about student achievement.

Level 1 (Low Level)

I know it's important to communicate effectively about student achievement, but I'm not sure the system I use does that. The idea of student involvement in assessment, record keeping, and communication is interesting, but I know little about it. I know it's important to communicate effectively about student achievement, but lack the time or know-how to do it.

Level 0 (Absence of Quality)

To motivate students I manage rewards and punishments. I am either opposed to student involvement in assessment or have no idea why it might be relevant or helpful. My record keeping system seems to meet my needs—I can assign grades every 10 weeks. I do not question whether traditional means of collecting, maintaining, summarizing, and delivering information about student achievement are meeting the needs of information users. I do not evaluate the effectiveness of my communication to see if the message is getting through.